PATCHWORK

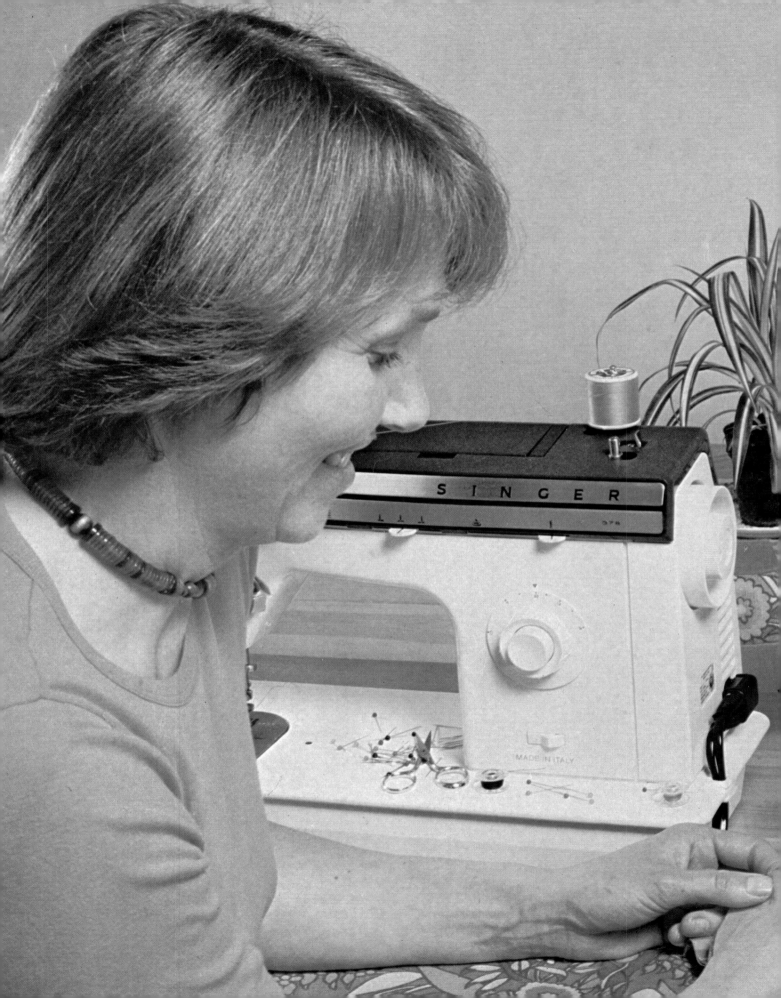

CREATIVE SEWING

PATCHWORK
MARY ANN GREEN

STUDIO VISTA / LONDON

A Studio Vista book published by
Cassell Ltd.,
35 Red Lion Square, London WC1R 4SG
and at Sydney, Auckland, Toronto, Johannesburg,
an affiliate of
Macmillan Publishing Co., Inc.,
New York

ISBN 0 289 70809 5

Designed by Reg Boorer

Artwork by Mary Ann Green and Denis Hawkins

Photography by Clive Corless,
(with Michael Buselle, David Cripps and Melvin Grey)

Published in association with The Singer Company (U.K.) Ltd

Printed by Sackville Press, Billericay Limited, Billericay, Essex

CONTENTS

Throughout this book,
measurements are supplied in
metric and imperial figures.
The two sets of figures
are not always exact equivalents, so
**follow one set of
measurements only.**

INTRODUCTION

Patchwork is an age-old craft, rich in tradition, and the designs in this book have been taken from the patterns developed long ago by our ancestors on both sides of the Atlantic. The projects featured have all been selected for their ease of construction and many can be adapted for the machine, thus ensuring a quick result and, I hope, a lot of fun.

Although most of the patterns were originally repeated to make a large design, as in quilt-making, I have tried to show that it is possible to select one motif and adapt it for use on a smaller scale. In this way, even the busiest needlewoman can make a place in the modern home for traditional ideas—a patchwork cushion or border for bedroom curtains, a gay smock or bag.

Success lies in the careful planning of a design before you begin. Once you have decided on your plan and chosen the colours, the patchwork can be made up quite simply and quickly.

MATERIAL
Almost all fabrics are suitable for patchwork, although cotton is the most popular because it will wash and wear well and consequently has a long life. Fine, heavy, textured or patterned material, even cotton velvet, will behave well provided the pieces put together are of similar weight. Felt, linen, silk, satin, lurex and closely woven wool can all be used. The beginner should be wary of man-made fibres as they do not fold well.

The materials to avoid are those that fray badly or stretch. Any secondhand fabric should be discarded, even if it appears to be sound. It will inevitably disintegrate long before the rest of the work and the wasted effort is heartbreaking.

All materials should be washed before use to prevent uneven shrinkage when you wash the

Left The traditional Sunburst pattern, on a quilt made in 1840.

1 All these fabrics are suitable for patchwork. Cottons are the most popular.

made-up article. This will also test the fastness of the dyes, and identify any colours that are going to 'bleed'. Two of the major culprits here are red and purple. Selvedges should be trimmed as they tend to pucker.

It is possible to mix fabrics, but this is not recommended for articles that will have a great deal of wear. The stronger pieces will eventually pull the weaker ones out of shape, and the work will never lie really flat.

Silks, satins and drip-dry cottons are easily marked by pins, so instead of pinning press the folds in place and tack through the seam allowance and paper only.

If your ragbag does not always yield the selection of colours required, it may be worth supplementing it with some bought pieces. Plain toning colours, for example, are often in short supply. If you have a hotchpotch of colours that do not look well together, try dyeing them all one colour. You will then have a range of toning shades which will look very subtle.

EQUIPMENT

Fortunately, the basic requirements for patchwork are not expensive. Most of the tools you need will already be in your needlework box.

As you assemble the patches, you will find that both neatness and strength are essential to prevent the work coming undone at points and corners. It is here that tension is lost, so often resulting in ugly stitches showing on the right side of the finished piece.

Needles

The seams must be closely sewn, and you should always use fine needles and thread. If you have difficulty in threading 'sharps', use a fine crewel needle which has a larger eye. An average guide for hand sewing is approximately 6 stitches within 1 cm (16 to the inch). On the machine, use a medium straight stitch.

Threads

For most patchwork use a fine mercerized cotton, as it will knot less than synthetic thread. Ideally, polyester or nylon thread should be used for fabrics containing man-made fibres, and always use silk to stitch silk. Use tacking cotton to construct the patches.

If possible, try to match the cotton to the basic colour of the work. Failing that, a black thread for dark patches and a white thread for light patches looks best. When sewing light material to dark, a black thread seems to show less. Invisible threads are now available, but as they are synthetic they are only really suitable for use on man-made material.

Scissors

You will need a sharp pair with points for cutting fabrics and for any unpicking. An old pair of scissors will do for the paper linings.

Pins

To avoid marking the fabric, always use good quality dressmakers' pins. For small work 'lills' or 'lillikins' are useful as they are tiny and will not get in the way.

Pencils

For marking out the fabric on the wrong side, use a medium-soft lead pencil. Never use a ballpoint pen as it will stain permanently. If you have to mark the material on the right side, use a special dressmakers' pencil.

Iron-on interlining

This will give weight to flimsy material and make it easier to handle. It can also be used in place of paper to make the patches for bags and boxes, as it can be left in the finished work.

Silk has a shorter lifespan than cotton or wool so it is a good idea to line it, particularly if it is used in conjunction with other fabrics. Many of the old silk quilts have survived because the pieces were lined.

Papers

The paper linings over which the fabric patches are made can be cut from any heavy paper: old Christmas cards, used business envelopes, postcards, brochures or even the covers of glossy magazines.

Work surface

A drawing board or sheet of cork is invaluable for planning your patchwork design. The pieces can be arranged, then pinned in place and left undisturbed until ready for use. It is often a good idea to lay out a design on the board and leave it propped up for a day or two where you can see it. You can then experiment with the colours to see if they work together, and if not rearrange them until you are satisfied. A separate board is wonderful for all of us that have only the dining room table to work on!

2 Work out your patchwork design on graph paper before cutting any material. This quilt (right) shows effective use of colour and planning.

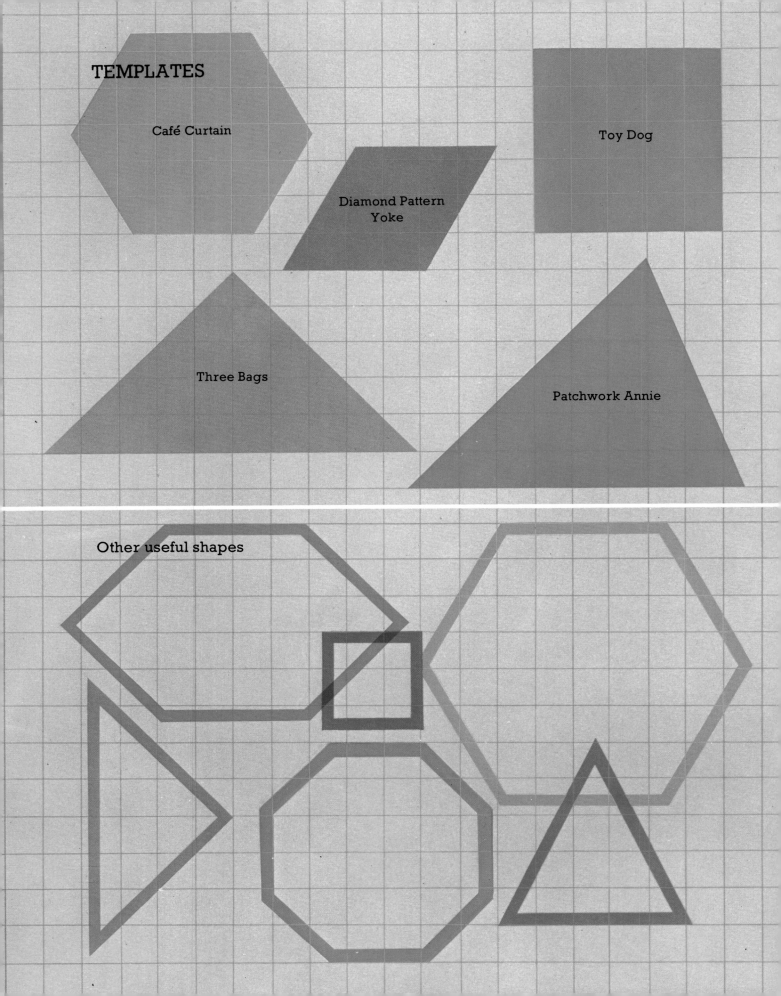

TEMPLATES

Café Curtain

Diamond Pattern
Yoke

Toy Dog

Three Bags

Patchwork Annie

Other useful shapes

TEMPLATES

These must be completely accurate or the small discrepancy at the centre of a piece of work can become a huge mistake by the time it reaches the edge, particularly if the work is quilt-sized. For this reason I recommend bought templates rather than home-made ones.

Packaged templates usually come in pairs: a solid metal shape for papers, and a plastic window from which the fabric patch is cut. They can be bought at any good needlework shop or by post from specialist suppliers, and come in a variety of shapes and sizes. The medium to large ones are best for a beginner, as very small sizes can be tricky to handle at first.

Do remember when ordering by post that templates are measured along the length of *one side,* not by the overall measurement.

The easiest shape to begin with is the familiar hexagon, as it has no sharp corners.

Making your own templates

If you find you are not able to buy ready-made templates, it is possible to make your own. A selection of shapes is given on page 10 and any of these can be traced off to serve as a pattern. Metal, perspex or plastic are the most durable materials to cut from. You can use a thick card but I do not recommend it for large projects; it wears away at the edges with constant use and may distort the shape of your design. The large, flat sides of the giant bottles containing washing-up liquid make perfect material for templates!

The equipment you will need for making templates is as follows:
plastic, thick card, metal sheet or perspex, metal ruler, protractor, set square, sharp handicraft knife, pencil.

Trace one of the shapes from page 10 onto card or plastic. Cut out along the drawn line, using a metal ruler and handicraft knife.

Any of these basic shapes can be made larger or smaller as long as the amount added or taken away is equal all round.

If the patchwork has a small geometric design and is to be made up on the machine, the only way to ensure complete accuracy is to use a specially made window template, which will allow both a cutting and a sewing line to be drawn on the fabric (**3**). Without this the corners and points of the design will not match.

To make a window template for machine work, draw the shape and size of the finished patch onto card or plastic. Leaving a 1 cm ($\frac{3}{8}$ in) border for the seam allowance, draw all round again. Cut out, using a metal ruler and handicraft knife.

3 Handmade window templates for machine work can be made out of thick card. You can also use thick plastic.

4 The window template helps you to select the precise piece of fabric that you need for the design, perhaps a leaf or a flower.

5 Draw round the window template. Use a soft pencil.

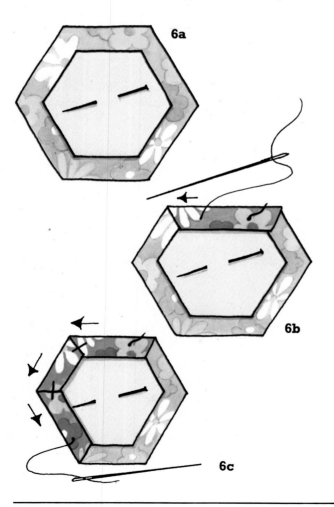

6a

6b

6c

MAKING THE PATCHES BY HAND

First cut the paper linings, using the solid template. Whatever shape you choose, this will represent the size of the finished patch and from this you can estimate the total number of patches you are going to need.

You can cut several paper linings at once if you first tear a strip of paper slightly wider than the solid template, and then fold it over lengthwise two or three times. Place the template in the centre of the folded paper, hold firmly and cut all round. To be absolutely accurate, let the scissor blades actually touch the template.

All the fabric patches must be cut on the straight grain of the material. This will prevent puckering and even though some seams are bound to be on the bias, as with two of the four sides of a diamond, if they are cut true it will help to keep the finished work flat.

Place the template on the material, with one edge in line with the grain, and lightly mark all round it with a pencil. Then cut along the pencil line. Try and stack your cut patches in groups of light and dark colours to save time later.

To make up the patches, pin the paper shape to the wrong side of the fabric patch (6a). Working from right to left, turn down the seam allowances (6b). Tack firmly through all thicknesses (6c). Check that the folds of the material fit exactly over the edges of the paper by pressing them with your fingers. This is very important at the corners, which must be true in shape.

Joining the patches

Take the first two patches and, with the right sides together, join them with fine oversewing. Take care not to stitch through the paper (7a) by only picking up two or three threads from each patch. No knots are necessary, just lay the thread along the top of the patches and stitch over it, working from right to left.

To fasten off, work back over the last few stitches several times. So much patchwork is badly fitted together, and on close inspection reveals badly sewn seams and little holes where the points should meet. To prevent this, stitch all seams towards a point, never away from one (7b).

6a Pin the paper shape to the wrong side of the fabric patch. 6b Turn down the seam allowance. 6c Tack firmly at corners, sewing through all thicknesses.

Finishing off

When all the patches have been sewn together, remove the tacking and press the work on the wrong side. Do not try to open the seams of hand-sewn work, but leave them turned to one side. Then remove the papers and press the work again on the right side under a damp cloth. If velvet features in the patchwork, use a needleboard to prevent flattening the pile. The work is now ready to be made-up.

The importance of pressing small units that are to be part of a larger design as you go along cannot be stressed enough.

Blindstitch

If the piece of work is to be mounted on a separate background, a blindstitch should be used (8). This is the neatest and most traditional stitch and, as its name suggests, is virtually invisible if the cotton matches the fabric.

MACHINE PATCHWORK

Any patch of 5 cm (2 in) or larger can easily be handled by the beginner and made up on the machine. Papers are not used and the fabric patches are made with the aid of a specially cut window template, with an open centre. This allows you to draw an inner line as a stitching guide, as well as the cutting line (4).

Stitch the patches together in strips of the required length. These can then be joined together to make up the design. Use a standard straight stitch, doubling back a few stitches at both ends of each seam to prevent the threads unravelling.

Random patchwork (9) can be made entirely on the sewing machine. Odd-sized pieces of material are seamed together in strips of equal width, and these in turn stitched together. The great advantage of this method is that you can make up a large area of patchwork quickly.

Press the seams of all machine patchwork open after stitching. If you are working on a large scale, and particularly if you are using a dark material, the seams can all be pressed in one direction as long as they do not show on the right side. When the work is completed, press it on the right side under a damp cloth.

7a Lay the thread along the top of the patches and stitch over, working from right to left. **7b** Stitch all seams towards a point to make a good corner.
8 Use blindstitch for appliqué.

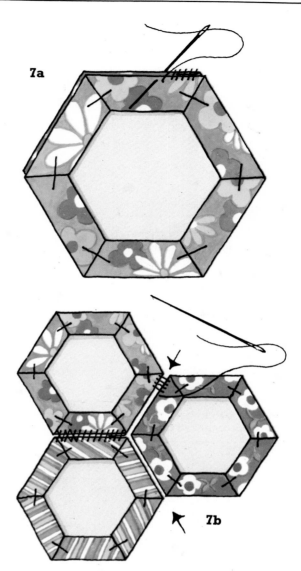

7a

7b

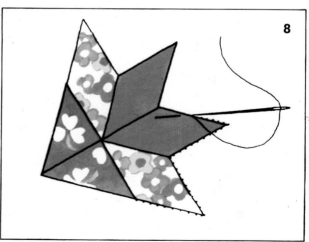

8

13

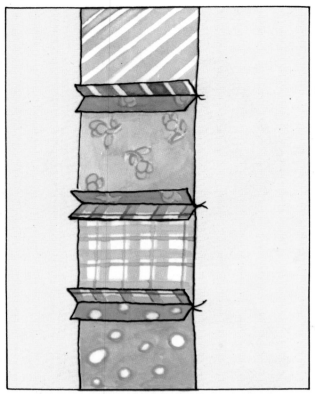

9 Machine patchwork: stitch the patches together in strips of the required length.

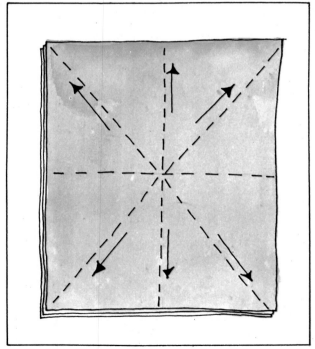

10 Tacking lines for lining and interlining a quilt. Work from the centre outwards.

LINING

Although patchwork, if well made, is very strong and hardwearing, it can become distorted if the grain does not run uniformly throughout. For this reason it is best to line any work that is to be made up as part of a garment.

If you want to quilt sections of clothing, insert a layer of fine synthetic wadding between the patchwork and the lining and topstitch chosen parts of the design. This will throw the patchwork into relief.

Interlining quilts

Nowadays synthetic wadding or cotton is used to pad quilts for extra warmth, a far cry from the heavy felted blankets and old flannelette sheets used in the past.

The interlining is sandwiched between the patchwork top and the lining, and all three thicknesses are stitched together at regular intervals. For most quilts use the thinnest terylene wadding, as the thicker the filling the more difficult it is to sew, particularly by machine. This manmade fibre has the advantage of being machinewashable and lightweight. Strips of interlining can be joined easily, without creating ridges, if you use a simple herringbone stitch.

Whether you are lining a cot cover or a double-bed-sized quilt, the process is the same. If possible, and particularly if the piece is large, clear all the furniture to one side and work on the floor.

Make up the lining to the required width and length, remembering that it should be at least 5 cm (2 in) larger all round than the finished patchwork top—the top will stretch as the wrinkles are pushed out to the edge. Press it well with the seams open and lay it on the floor, wrong side up. Position the wadding on top of the lining, and on top of that the patchwork, right side up. Using weights, pins and any help you can get, smooth and straighten until all the edges correspond.

Now, tack through all three thicknesses, *starting from the centre and working outwards*. First make a cross of tacking stitches in the centre of the quilt, then take diagonal lines out to the four corners (**10**). Working by this method, any wrinkles will be pushed outwards to the edge and eventually lost. When that is done, tack round the outer edge. Your quilt is now ready to be quilted and bound.

COLOUR

Although colour is usually chosen by instinct, a basic knowledge of the spectrum will help you when you are making the final selection of fabrics for a design (**11**). There are no absolute rules, for much will depend on your own personal reaction to colour. Nevertheless some understanding of what it can do will give you an idea of where to start.

Plan your design to balance the different strengths of colour. You will find that the colours from the warm side of the spectrum usually stand out, while the ones from the cooler side recede. (This can be reversed by varying the intensity of the bluer hues and making the warm colours very pale.)

Size does not always equal strength, and a small patch of red can be as intense as a larger area. See how the same patch appears to change, depending on whether its neighbour is yellow or blue (**12**). Once you have grasped this, you can introduce movement into a design by putting together contrasting tones which will be more dynamic than those of similar intensity.

Understanding the properties of each colour will help you to choose fabric because of what it can do for your design, rather than for itself alone. Choose colours in the same light they will be seen in when they are made up, for some materials change radically under artificial light. The reds usually become dull, and the blues and greens more vivid.

Don't be frightened to experiment, for the creative potential is enormous. But do remember that a random choice of materials is rarely as effective as a well-thought-out and balanced design containing a limited number of colours, say three or four (**13**).

Gradually, as you begin to understand what can be done with shape and colour, you can begin to introduce texture. The softness of velvet or the brightness of satin can completely alter the effect.

Patterned fabrics can be used together, but try to vary the emphasis so that the small flowers of one patch appear against the larger design of another. Intersperse patterns with plain fabric, which will act as a foil to the more detailed pieces.

Finally, don't try to be too clever. Keep your design simple, with a good balance of light and dark.

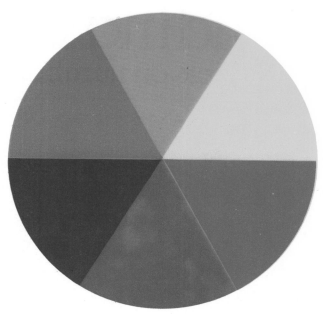

11 The spectrum.

12 See how one colour can appear to change another. The red is exactly the same colour.

13 Experiment with colour arrangements before finally stitching fabrics together.

Building Bricks
with stick-on numbers

1 With right sides together and using the pencil line as a guide, machine the four sides of the brick to the centre patch.

2 Cut six different numbers from contrasting felt. Centre one carefully on each side of the brick and fix in place with a latex glue.

For each brick, you will need:
38 cm x 25 cm (15 in x 10 in) felt in main colour
23 cm x 23 cm (9 in x 9 in) square of felt in contrasting colour, for numbers
Tracing paper, latex glue, stuffing
Thick card, metal ruler and handicraft knife, for making template

The square patch is the easiest to use, whether it is to be made up into a piece of material or into a three-dimensional object. These bricks can be made up very quickly on the machine.

The quality of felt varies a great deal, so if you cannot find one of reasonable weight you might need to back the thinner ones with an iron-on interlining. Buy the same quantity of interlining as felt. Iron on the lining before cutting out each brick. The numbers can also be treated in this way to prevent any glue seeping through less substantial fabrics.

To make each brick
Cut a 10 cm (4 in) square template from thick card. Working on the wrong side of the larger piece of felt, draw round the template. Cut out the patch, leaving a 7 mm ($\frac{1}{4}$ in) seam allowance all round for turnings. Cut six patches altogether.

Arrange four of the patches round one centre patch, ready for sewing (**1**). With right sides together, pin each patch in turn to the centre one. Machine along the pencil line, leaving the 7 mm ($\frac{1}{4}$ in) free at each end. Double back on all seams a few stitches to secure. Pin and sew each of the four patches to its neighbour.

Pin the sixth side of the brick in place. Machine round on three sides only. Turn to right side. Stuff firmly and close the remaining seam with small stitches.

Numbers
Trace off the number shapes from page 60. Cut six numbers from contrasting felt and fix one to each side of the brick, using a latex glue (**2**).

Three Bags
all made from one template

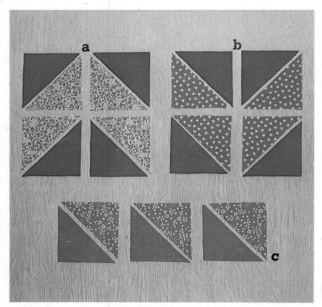

1 Layout for **a** workbag, **b** child's purse, **c** clutch bag. Each bag has a different arrangement of plain and print triangles. Machine each pair of triangles together to make a square.

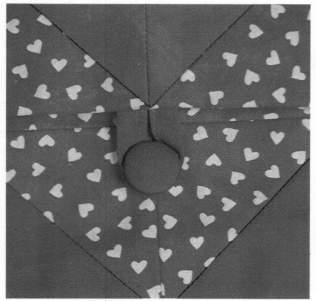

2 Cover the button base in matching fabric and sew in place opposite the loop.

These three bags are all made on the machine and use the same window template, based on a right-angled triangle. Each of the designs is made up from different arrangements of light and dark triangles, which are stitched together to form a square. These squares were originally sewn together in a long strip and used as a border for edging the old American quilts. The alternating light and dark triangle design was appropriately known as 'Sawtooth'.

CHILD'S SHOULDER PURSE
You will need:
15 cm (6 in) of 90 cm (36 in) width material in plain colour

15 cm (6 in) of 90 cm (36 in) width material in print

20 cm ($\frac{1}{4}$ yd) of 90 cm (36 in) width material in contrast colour, for lining, button loop and binding

One 2 cm ($\frac{3}{4}$ in) button base

Approx 5.50 m (6 yd) chunky wool

Tracing paper, thick card, metal ruler and handicraft knife, for making template

Template
Trace the right-angled triangle from page 10 and transfer to card. To construct a window template, draw a 1 cm ($\frac{3}{8}$ in) seam allowance all round. Using a sharp knife and ruler, cut out along both the inside and outside lines (see page 11).

Patchwork
Using your template as a guide and marking both cutting and stitching lines, cut 10 plain patches and 10 print patches. Make sure the right angle of the triangle is in line with the grain of the fabric. Alternate triangles to economize on material (see page 34).

Lay the patches on a board in pairs of plain and print, making five lines of four patches each. The chevron effect is made by alternating the colours (**1b**).

With right sides facing, machine along the

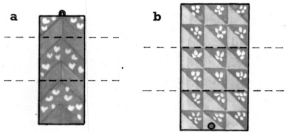

a   b

3 Fold along the dotted lines for **a** child's purse **b** clutch bag.

4 Adjust the woollen cord to the required length.

5 Finish the clutch bag with red binding.

drawn line to make each pair of triangles into a square. Double back two or three stitches at each end to secure. Press seams open and return each square to the correct position on the board.

Now join the two squares of each line together. Working from top to bottom, machine the five strips together. Press seams open, then press whole patchwork section well under a damp cloth.

Loop
Cut a strip of contrast material 9 cm x 3.5 cm (3½ in x 1¼ in). Press the raw edges into the centre. Fold in half lengthways and topstitch. Double over into loop. Tack firmly to right side of patchwork at top centre seam (see page 28).

Lining
Cut a piece of contrast material 16 cm x 38 cm (6½ in x 15 in). With right sides together, machine lining to patchwork at top and bottom. Turn to right side and press. With wrong side facing you, fold the bottom section over (**3a**). Tack in position.

Binding and button
Cut two lengths of contrast fabric 24 cm x 4 cm (9½ in x 1½ in). With right sides together, tack the binding along one long edge of the purse, leaving a 1 cm (⅜ in) seam. Machine. Turn binding over edge. Trim and turn in two short ends. Press under a 1 cm (⅜ in) seam and hem down. Repeat for other side.

Cover the button base with plain material. Line up with loop and stitch in place (**2**).

Cord
Plait or twist the wool to make a thick cord. Knot and fringe each end (**4**), adjusting the length if necessary. Slipstitch to back of purse, attaching the cord down each side.

CLUTCH BAG
You will need:
30 cm (12 in) of 90 cm (36 in) width material in plain colour
30 cm (12 in) of 90 cm (36 in) width material in flowered print
25 cm (9 in) of 90 cm (36 in) width material in contrast colour, for lining and binding
One 2 cm (¾ in) button base (optional)
Materials for making template, as above

Patchwork

Construct a window template, as above, under Child's Shoulder Purse. Using your template as above, cut 18 plain patches and 18 print patches. Arrange the patches in pairs of plain and print (**1c**). Join the pairs of triangles into squares (see above).

Arrange the squares in lines of three (**1c**), with all the print triangles on the same side. Join the three squares of each line together. Machine the six strips together into one piece of patchwork (**3b**).

Lining

Cut a piece of contrast material 23 cm x 45 cm (9 in x 18 in). Machine lining and turn bag as above.

Binding and button

Cut two lengths of contrast fabric 30 cm x 3.5 cm (12 in x 1¼ in). Bind as the child's purse, but use a slightly smaller seam to give a narrower edge (**5**).

Cover the button base in contrast material. Stitch to either the centre or the side of the flap. Secure with a press stud on the underside of the flap.

WORKBAG WITH WOODEN HANDLES

You will need:

90 cm (1 yd) of 90 cm (36 in) width material in plain colour
90 cm (1 yd) of 90 cm (36 in) width material in print
45 cm (18 in) of 90 cm (36 in) width material in contrast colour, for lining
One pair wooden handles
Materials for making template, as above

Patchwork

Construct a window template, as above, under Child's Shoulder Purse. Using your template as above, cut 72 plain patches and 72 print patches. Arrange the patches in pairs of plain and print (**1a**). Join the pairs of triangles into squares (see above).

Divide the squares into two groups of 36, for the front and back of the bag. Arrange 36 patches in a block of six by six. Make a chevron design by alternating the plain and print edges right across each line (**1a**).

Join the squares together in strips, then machine the strips together, as above. Repeat with the remaining 36 patches for the back of the bag.

To make up bag

With right sides together, machine two halves of bag together at bottom. Machine side seams for 28 cm (11 in) only. Turn bag to right side.

Cut two strips of plain fabric 9 cm x 43 cm (3½ in x 17 in). With right sides together, machine to each side of bag at the top, leaving a 1 cm (⅜ in) seam. Press under side seam. Topstitch all round each side opening to strengthen.

Handles

Pass the strips of plain material through the wooden handles. Fold to inside of bag and pin level with top of patchwork. Tack in place, checking that both handles are level. Topstitch on right side.

Lining

Fold lining fabric in half widthways. Pin side seams, checking against patchwork for size. Trim excess material. Machine side seams for 28 cm (11 in). Do not turn.

With wrong sides together, drop lining into bag, matching side openings and corners. Turn under excess fabric at top and pin below handle. Slipstitch in position all round (**6**).

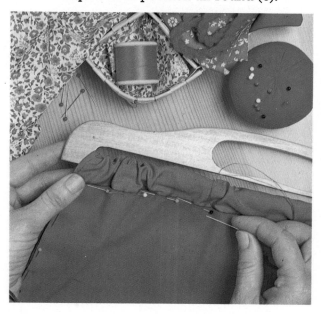

6 To complete the workbag pin the lining in place, matching the side openings. Slipstitch in position.

Toy Dog
made up in simple squares

1 Arrange the patches for the side of the dog in lines. Machine them into strips and return to the board so you see the dog's shape as you work.

2 Cut the dog's features from scraps of felt and his inner ears from a matching cotton lining. The tail and nose sections are stuffed.

You will need:
Scraps of material in bold, simple prints
Scraps of felt in black, white and yellow
1 bag of stuffing, approx. 400 gm (1 lb) in weight
Latex glue
Thick card, metal ruler and handicraft knife, for making template

The body of the dog can be made entirely on the machine and the features glued and hand-stitched in place to finish. You can use a mixture of similar-weight fabrics, including needlecord and felt.

Template
Construct one square window template from card (see page 11), with an inner size of 5 cm (2 in) and an outer size of 7 cm (2¾ in). This gives a 1 cm (⅜ in) seam allowance all round.

With the aid of your template and drawing both an outer and inner line, cut 70 patches: 22 for each side of the dog and 26 for the gusset. Arrange them in lines ready for stitching (**1**).

To make dog
Using your drawn inner line as a guide and working from left to right, machine the top row of three patches together. Press all seams open as you go. Repeat with the remaining rows, working from top to bottom of the dog. Return each row to its place on the board so that you can always see the shape of the animal.

Starting with the head, with right sides together and working down the body, machine the rows of patches together into one piece of fabric. Press well. Repeat with the 22 patches for the second side.

Make up the remaining 26 patches into one long strip. This will form the centre gusset. With right sides together and starting at the back leg, pin and tack the length of gusset to one of the body pieces. Ease gently at all corners and clip where necessary. Machine in

3 Sew the ears to the head at the seamline.

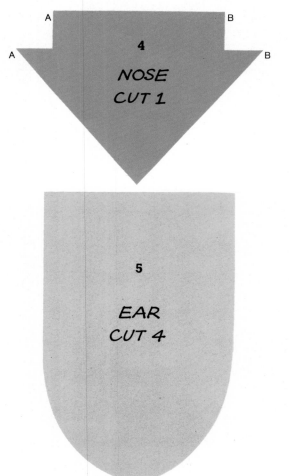

place. (You may find it difficult to manoeuvre the material at the corners, in which case the gusset can be set in by hand, using a small backstitch.)

Repeat with the second body piece, leaving the back three patches open. Turn the dog to the right side and stuff. Fill the head first, then the feet, pushing the stuffing well into the corners with a knitting needle. When firm, close the opening with slipstitch.

Features

Eyes. Cut two circles 2.5 cm (1 in) across from black felt. Cut two white crescents and glue in place (**2**).

Nose. Trace the pattern (**4**) and cut one nose piece from black felt. Close points A and points B together with oversewing on the wrong side. Fit the nose over the dog's snout and stitch down, padding lightly before completing the last few stitches.

Ears. Using the pattern (**5**), cut four ear pieces. With right sides facing, machine together in two pairs all round curved edge. Turn to right side, turning in straight edge. Press. Stitch to top of head at seamline (**3**).

Tail. Cut a triangle of felt 13 cm (5 in) high and with a 10 cm (4 in) base. Fold in half lengthways and machine down the long edge. Turn to right side. Stuff firmly and stitch to dog on the top back patch of gusset.

6 The dog is firm enough to stand upright.

Café Curtain
in traditional hexagon design

The hexagon, or honeycomb, is one of the most popular patchwork shapes. Its wide angles and lack of sharp corners make it ideal for the beginner.

Seven hexagons joined together make a single flower or 'rose'. Made into quilts (1) the design has many names, including Grandmother's Flower Garden and French Bouquet.

The hexagon motif can also be made into a diamond-shaped block and used singly, as on these placemats, or strung together as the border design on the café curtain.

CURTAIN
You will need:
1 m (1 yd) of 90 cm (36 in) width plain cotton
70 cm ($\frac{3}{4}$ yd) of 115 cm (45 in) width curtain lining in matching colour
45 cm (18 in) of 90 cm (36 in) width small-check gingham
10 cm (4 in) of 90 cm (36 in) width large-check gingham
One 3.5 cm ($1\frac{1}{4}$ in) solid template hexagon shape, and one 4.5 cm ($1\frac{3}{4}$ in) window template, hexagon shape (these can be bought as a pair) **or** thick card, metal ruler and handicraft knife for making your own template (see pages 10 and 11)
Thick paper, for making paper linings
Brass or wooden curtain rod and brackets, to fit individual window

This amount of fabric is to fit a window 86 cm x 61 cm (34 in x 24 in). Measure the width of your window and the drop from the curtain rod to the sill. Add 3 cm (1 in) to the width and 8 cm (3 in) to the length.

Trim selvedges to prevent puckering and cut fabric to required size. Turn up a 2.5 cm (1 in) double hem along the bottom and machine. Prepare the lining to match.

Patchwork
Using window template, cut six patches from

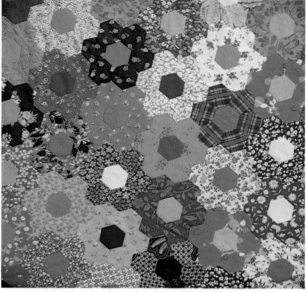

1 The flowers for this random design are made from bright prints contrasting with plain centres.

small-check gingham and one from large check. Using solid template, cut paper linings.

Make up each patch (see page 12) and stitch together to form a flower motif of seven patches (2). Make four flowers in all.

Make an extra five patches from the large check gingham and stitch between each flower (2), linking them together to form a border. Press on wrong side. Remove tacking and press on right side before removing papers.

To mount border
Line up the border 7 cm ($2\frac{1}{2}$ in) from lower edge of curtain. Centre carefully. Pin and tack in place. Blindstitch (see page 13). Press.

To make curtain
With right sides together, pin lining to curtain at side seams, leaving a 1.5 cm ($\frac{1}{2}$ in) seam allowance. The lining should be slightly shorter than the curtain. Machine and press. Turn to right side and press side seams.

2 Make the flower motif into a diamond shape.

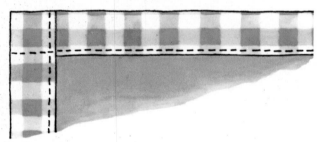

3 Topstitch the border hem of the mat.

4 The completed placemat.

Loops

The quantities given are for five loops.

From remaining plain fabric, cut ten rectangles each 10 cm x 15 cm (4 in x 6 in). On bias of material cut ten strips of gingham binding, each 15 cm (6 in) long and 3 cm (1¼ in) wide.

Pin two of the rectangles wrong sides together. Bind both long edges with gingham (see page 50), allowing only 7 mm (¼ in) turning to give a dainty edge. Repeat for remaining loops.

Turn in and press the top edge of curtain and lining, making the length 6 cm (2¼ in) less than the finished drop. Place one end of each loop between the curtain and lining, leaving a 1½ cm (¾ in) seam. Position all loops so that they are equidistant, the outside two loops level with the curtain edges. Tack loops to curtain material, and machine along complete width of curtain with a row of topstitching.

Fold the loops over and tuck remaining ends between curtain and lining. Slipstitch lining in place.

PLACEMATS

For six mats, you will need:

1 m (1 yd) of 90 cm (36 in) width plain cotton
1.70 m (1¾ yd) of 90 cm (36 in) width small-check gingham
20 cm (¼ yd) of 90 cm (36 in) width large-check gingham
Templates and paper linings, as for curtain

Each mat measures 30 cm x 38 cm (12 in x 15 in).

Patchwork

For each mat, cut a 30 cm x 38 cm (12 in x 15 in) rectangle from plain material and a 35 cm x 43 cm (14 in x 17 in) rectangle from small-check gingham.

Make up a flower motif as above, adding an extra patch at either end to make a diamond shape (**2**). Appliqué the patchwork to the centre of the plain rectangle.

To make up mat

With wrong sides together, centre mat on gingham backing, leaving a 2.5 cm (1 in) gingham border all round. Tack together. Press under gingham border on all four sides to make a narrow hem. Turn border over edge of mat. Machine border with a row of topstitching (**3**).

Tabard
in random patchwork

1 Cut all strips in line with the grain of the fabric. Alternate light and dark tones. You can add ribbons on top for extra colour.

2 Lay the centre line of the pattern pieces along the fold of the patchwork.

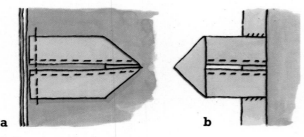

a   b

3 How to make the loops.

You will need:

Strips of furnishing-weight cotton, in toning plain and print colours

1.20 m (1½ yd) of 90 cm (36 in) width dress-weight cotton, in a plain colour, for lining

Toning ribbon (optional)

55 cm (22 in) of 97 cm (38 in) width lightweight terylene wadding

Ten 1.5 cm (½ in) diameter button bases

Dressmaker's pattern paper

Using dressmaker's paper, scale up the pattern from page 61. Make any alterations in size.

Cut a selection of strips 56 cm (22 in) in length and varying in width from 4.5 cm (1¾ in) to 8 cm (3 in) (**1**). Leaving a 1 cm (⅜ in) seam allowance on each strip, make up two pieces of random patchwork 51 cm x 56 cm (20 in x 22 in). Press all seams open.

Fold the patchwork in half lengthways and pin the front and back pattern pieces in place (**2**). Cut out and staystitch all round.

To make up tabard

Using the same pattern, cut two lining pieces 2.5 cm (1 in) larger all round. Cut two wadding pieces the same size.

With wrong sides together, pin all three thicknesses together along the seamlines. Quilt on the right side, machining a row of topstitching through all thicknesses, 3 mm (⅛ in) from each seamline. Work from the centre outwards. Trim excess lining and wadding.

Make 10 loops in lining fabric (see page 20). Fold each loop to form a point at the end (**3a**). Tack the loops to the underside of the tabard front, as marked on the pattern and pointing towards the centre. Stitch across ends.

From the remaining lining, cut bias strips 4 cm (1½ in) wide. Join to the required length, and with right sides facing, pin all round edge of tabard. Machine, leaving a 1 cm (⅜ in) seam. Turn over and hem down by hand. Press loops outwards and stitch down (**3b**).

Cover the button bases and stitch in place.

Log Cabin Quilt
a traditional American design

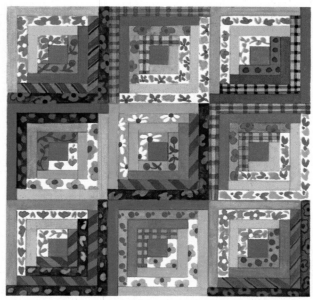

1 A variation of the basic Log Cabin design. This arrangement is known as Straight Furrow.

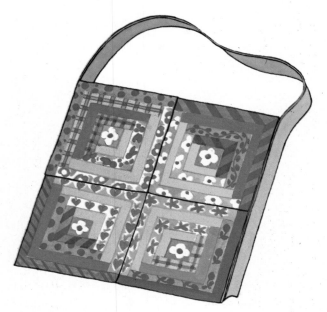

2 The blocks can be used singly or in pairs to make up the required size.

You will need:

70 cm (1 yd) of 90 cm (36 in) width dressweight material in plain colour, for centre squares
Approx. 13.50 m (15 yd) of 90 cm (36 in) width cotton materials in equal amounts of light and dark, including both patterned and plain
8.10 m (9 yd) of 90 cm (36 in) width natural calico, for foundation squares
8.10 m (9 yd) of 90 cm (36 in) width dressweight cotton, for lining
90 cm (1 yd) of 90 cm (36 in) width cotton in contrasting colour, for binding **or** approx. 10 m (10¾ yd) of purchased bias binding
7.30 m (8½ yd) of 97 cm (38 in) width lightweight terylene wadding (optional)

Log Cabin became very popular on both sides of the Atlantic during the latter half of the nineteenth century. Being a geometric design, it was easy to adapt to the sewing machine which came into domestic use at that time.

The design represents the overlapping logs of a wooden cabin with the fire in the centre. The light half of the block is the firelit side of the room and the dark strips the shadows. Some of the older quilts had a chimney added to the design.

The amounts given above are for a double-bed sized quilt, finished size 252 cm (96 in) square (12 x 12 blocks). Each block measures 23 cm (9 in) square.

Preparation of fabric
Pre-shrink all fabric, including calico, and iron well. Sort into light and dark shades.

Template
Make a drawn template to act as a guide and show the finished size. First draw a 23 cm (9 in) square. Mark diagonal lines from corner to corner and a 5 cm (2 in) square in the centre. Draw four 'steps', each 2 cm (¾ in) deep below the centre square and extending to the diagonal lines on either side (3). The 1 cm (½ in) remaining all round is the seam allowance.

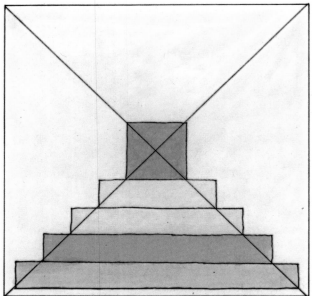

3 Use this template as a guide to the finished size of the 'logs'.

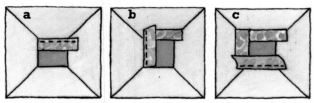

4 Machine the first row of two light and two dark logs in position over the centre square.

5 The first row of logs in position.

To make one block

Cut a 23 cm (9 in) square of calico for the foundation square. Mark the diagonals, either with tacking cotton or a soft lead pencil.

From the material chosen for the centre 'fire', cut a 6 cm x 6 cm ($2\frac{1}{2}$ in x $2\frac{1}{2}$ in) square. Tack to the centre of the calico base, right sides up. *First row.* Using the drawn steps as a guide, cut two light and two dark strips 3 cm ($1\frac{1}{4}$ in) deep and the exact length of the first step on the template. With right sides together, place the first light strip on the centre square, matching raw edges at one corner. It will extend beyond the square at the opposite end. Machine through all thicknesses, giving a 5 mm ($\frac{1}{4}$ in) seam allowance (**4a**). Turn strip to right side and press flat.

With right sides together, tack the second light strip to the centre square. Match raw edges and extend the second strip over the short end of the first strip (**4b**). Stitch. Turn to right side and press.

Using the same method, attach the two dark strips to the base square (**4c** and **5**).

Complete the block in this way, adding one row of two light and two dark strips at a time, 16 strips in all.

When cutting the strips for the fourth outer row, make them 3.5 cm ($1\frac{1}{2}$ in) deep and 23 cm (9 in) long to bring them out to the edge of the block.

To complete the quilt

Press all the blocks well and arrange with light and dark sides alternating, as opposite. Using a 1 cm ($\frac{1}{2}$ in) seam allowance, join the blocks into rows of 12, working across the quilt. Tack and sew the rows together.

You can now line and interline the quilt and bind it with a contrasting colour (see pages 14 and 50).

Right The Log Cabin block looks very effective repeated on a large scale, as in this quilt. Made in America in 1860, it shows a subtle combination of printed dress cottons. The 'logs' are outlined by quilting, which accentuates the design.

Friendship Ring Mats
to make from offcuts

1 The same design made in a different colour scheme and used to decorate a bolster end. The centre circle of the ring can be lightly padded and buttoned.

2 Working on the wrong side of the material, draw round the template. Remember to mark both the cutting and the stitching lines.

For two mats, you will need:
20 cm (12 in) of 90 cm (36 in) width dressweight material, in each of four toning prints (try to have a mixture of light and dark)
90 cm (36 in) of 90 cm (36 in) width material in plain, contrasting colour, for background
Tracing paper, thick card, metal ruler and handicraft knife, for making template

As many as 20 different prints may go to make up one circle, hence the name Friendship Ring as the maker usually had to call upon her friends to supply some of the materials. I have limited my number of fabrics to four, all within the blue-green colour range, but if you wish the circles may be made entirely from assorted scraps.

This design is very easy to make as the petals of the ring can be made up on the machine, and then appliquéd to the background fabric. The completed mats are approximately 35 cm (14 in) square.

Template
Trace the window template given overleaf and transfer to card. Using your handicraft knife and metal ruler, cut out, taking great care that the points of the actual 'window' are accurate (see page 11).

Patchwork
Using your window template as a guide and marking both the cutting and stitching lines on the wrong side of the material, cut 20 petals from the mixture of cotton prints (**2**). Make sure that one long edge of the template is in line with the grain of the fabric.

Arrange the petals on a board, alternating light and dark colours ready for sewing. With right sides facing, machine the first two petals together along the stitching line, working from the base of each petal outwards and stopping 1 cm ($\frac{3}{8}$ in) short of the outer edge (**3**). Double back over two or three stitches at both ends of the seam to secure. Add the remaining

3 Machine the 20 petals together to make a ring.

4 On the wrong side, turn in and tack down the seam allowance all round the outer edge of the ring.

petals, pressing all seams open as you go. It is easier if the circle is made up in two separate halves and these finally joined together.

On wrong side, turn down and tack 1 cm ($\frac{3}{8}$ in) all round the outer edge of the ring (**4**).

From one of the remaining prints, cut a circle 9 cm ($3\frac{1}{2}$ in) in diameter for the centre. Turn in by pressing 7 mm ($\frac{1}{4}$ in) all round the edge. Position in the centre of the ring of petals, covering the raw edges. Stitch in place.

To make mats
Trim selvedges off the background fabric, to prevent puckering. For each mat, cut two pieces of fabric 37 cm (15 in) square. Centre the ring of petals, with right sides up, on one of these squares. Make sure both layers of fabric lie flat, then tack in position. Blindstitch in place (see page 13).

With right sides facing, pin the two squares of the mat together. Machine stitch all round, leaving a 10 cm (4 in) opening on one side for turning. Turn to right side and press the edges and corners well. Close the opening with slipstitch.

Variations
This design can be echoed by a circular background, perhaps made up in velvets and used as a bolster end (**1**). The centre circle can be padded and buttoned.

Needlework Basket
with quilted lining

You will need:
Wicker workbasket with detachable lid, and a base approx. 23 cm (9 in) in diameter
Scraps of any number of toning cotton fabrics in light and dark shades
30 cm (12 in) of 97 cm (38 in) width lightweight terylene wadding
Compass, tracing paper, metal ruler, thick card and handicraft knife, for making template

A quilted lining gives a plain sewing basket an expensive look. This design uses the Dresden Plate motif for the base and lid, and random patchwork for the sides. The centre of the lid is padded and serves as a pincushion (**1**).

To make the pattern
Measure the diameter of the base of the basket, add 2 cm ($\frac{3}{4}$ in) seam allowance. Using a compass, draw a circle of this size onto tracing paper. Draw a smaller circle in the centre 4 cm ($1\frac{1}{2}$ in) across. The full circle will divide into 20 equal parts, each having an angle of 18°. This pattern will act as a guide for both patchwork and wadding, also for any alteration in size to the template.

Template
Trace the window template overleaf and transfer to card. Cut out carefully, using a handicraft knife. The pattern given is for a basket with a 23 cm (9 in) base. Should it need adjusting, lay the tracing of the template over the paper pattern, carefully matching the inner base line of the segment to the edge of the small circle. The two long sides of the template can be either lengthened or shortened to fit your own pattern.

Using the template as a guide and keeping one long edge in line with the grain, cut 20 patches from assorted fabrics. Draw both cutting and stitching lines on the wrong side of the fabric. Lay out the design ready for sewing. With right sides facing and using the pencil line as a guide, machine two segments

1 The centre circle of the lid is padded to make a pincushion.

2 Quilt alternate patches by machining two rows of topstitching through all the thicknesses, 3 mm ($\frac{1}{8}$ in) from each seamline. Work from the centre outwards to prevent puckering.

together. Press seam open. Repeat with remaining patches to complete the circle.

To quilt the lining
Cut a circle of the same size from synthetic

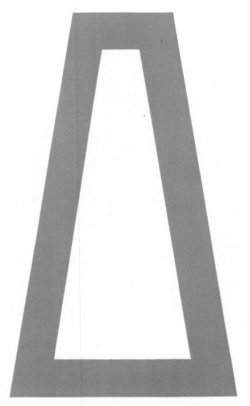

3 Tack down outer edge of patchwork circle.

wadding. Tack to the underside of the patchwork. Working on the right side and on alternate patches, machine two rows of topstitching through both thicknesses 3 mm ($\frac{1}{8}$ in) from each seamline (**2**). Machine from the centre out to prevent puckering, and use either a matching or contrasting thread. Cut a circle of fabric 9 cm (3$\frac{1}{2}$ in) across. Press in 5 mm ($\frac{1}{4}$ in) all round the edge. Position in centre of patchwork, covering raw edges. Stitch in place. Finish with a row of topstitching.

Sides of lining
Measure the circumference of the basket. Using matching fabrics, machine together a strip of random-size pieces to this length and 3 cm (1$\frac{1}{4}$ in) wider than the depth of the basket (see page 13).

Cut a strip of wadding to the same length and the exact depth of the basket. Tack the two together, matching one long edge. Quilt by topstitching each alternate patch, as for the base. With right sides facing, seam the two short ends together.

Pin and tack the base to the side lining, with right sides together. Make any adjustments in fitting now. If the basket has slanting sides, gather any excess into the base seam with tiny pleats. Machine together. Turn the patchwork over the edge of the wadding at the top and tack down to wadding only. Position lining in basket. Stitch in place by taking the thread through the gaps in the wicker and catching the top edge of the lining, at intervals of 2 cm ($\frac{3}{4}$ in). The stitches will be invisible if worked under the rim of the basket.

To line the lid
Using the same template, make a circle of patchwork 2 cm ($\frac{3}{4}$ in) bigger than the inside of the lid. (If the lid is larger than the base, alter the template as previously described). Cut a circle of wadding to fit the lid exactly. Tack the two together and quilt as for the base. Turn the outer edge of the patchwork over the wadding and tack down to wadding only (**3**).

Cut a circle of fabric 9 cm (3$\frac{1}{2}$ in) in diameter. Turn in by pressing 1 cm ($\frac{3}{8}$ in) all round. Cut three 7 cm (2$\frac{3}{4}$ in) circles from the wadding. Tack to underside of fabric circle to make a padded pincushion. Centre the cushion over raw edges of patchwork and hem down (**1**). Place lining in lid and attach as for sides.

House-on-the-Hill Bag
in two different colour schemes

1 Arrange the fabric pieces in their lines ready for sewing. For this version of the bag, the toy bag, one roof section and one house section have been subdivided.

2 Frame the house block with a contrasting border before making it up into a bag.

You will need:
Scraps of light material for the sky, in assorted colours
Scraps of dark material, for the house
32 cm x 9.5 cm (12½ in x 4 in) flower print material, for the hill
50 cm (¾ yd) of 90 cm (36 in) width material, for the back of bag, handles and border round house
50 cm (¾ yd) of 90 cm (36 in) width contrasting fabric, for the lining
Tracing paper

This pattern, one of the most naturalistic of the American house or cabin designs, makes up into a 30 cm x 30 cm (11¾ in x 11¾ in) block. If possible keep the largest flower print for the hill piece. The pieces can be appliquéd onto a coloured background or pieced together by machine.

Each section of the pattern can be divided in two again to add another colour to the house. The toy bag and the needlework bag (overleaf) show two different adaptations of the same basic pattern. The toy bag contains four patterned materials and one plain colour. The needlework bag has a more complex mixture of six patterns and one plain.

When assembled, the block is framed by a 5 cm (2 in) border (**2**).

To make the house
Trace the pattern sections from page 62 and cut them out carefully. Always line up one edge of each pattern piece with the grain of the fabric. Allow a 1 cm (½ in) seam allowance all round each section.

Arrange the fabric pieces on a board. They will fall naturally into four strips (**1** and **4**).

Beginning with the top line and working from left to right, join all the sky and chimney pieces into a strip. Press all seams open as you go. Repeat for the other three sections.

When all four strips are complete seam them together, working from top to bottom. Press.

3 Secure the handles and join the lining to the toy bag with two rows of decorative topstitching.

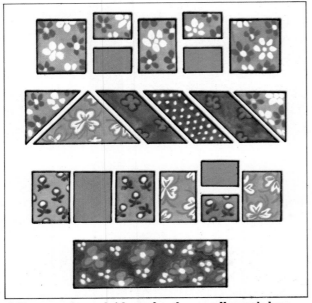

4 Pattern pieces laid out for the needlework bag.

5 To make the needlework bag, add a 9 cm (3½ in) border at the top and gather the bag onto the handles.

Border

Cut two pieces 7 cm x 30 cm (3 in x 12 in) and two pieces 7 cm x 42 cm (3 in x 17 in) from main fabric. With right sides together and leaving a 1 cm (½ in) seam, machine the two short pieces to the top and bottom of the house block. Open outwards and press.

Repeat with the two long side borders. Press.

Cut a 42 cm x 42 cm (17 in x 17 in) square of main fabric. With right sides together and leaving a 1 cm (½ in) seam, machine to the house block on three sides, leaving top side open. Turn right side out. Fold a 1 cm (½ in) hem in round the top of the bag and pin.

Handles

Cut two pieces 40 cm x 7 cm (16 in x 3 in) from main fabric. With right sides facing, fold the strips lengthways and machine. Turn right side out and press, with the seam in the centre. Finish with two rows of topstitching.

With wrong sides facing inwards, pin the handles to the inside of the bag. The ends should be 18 cm (7 in) apart. Tack to the turned-in hem at the top of the bag.

Lining

Cut a lining 42 cm x 84 cm (17 in x 34 in). Fold in half, with right sides together. Machine side seams. Turn down a 1 cm (½ in) hem on the wrong side and tack. Drop the lining into the bag, matching up the top edges. Tack all round through both thicknesses, taking care to secure the handles. Topstitch all round on the machine, using a contrasting cotton (**3**). Do two rows.

Variations

As this design makes up into a block, it would also be suitable as a quilt design, particularly for a child's room. If you are making a large piece such as a quilt, you will need to make window templates (see page 11) as the paper tracing would not last long.

Sunburst Cushion
with piped edge

You will need:

Four co-ordinating dressweight fabrics, with one colour predominating

20 cm (¼ yd) of 90 cm (36 in) width material in main colour, for centre and piping

20 cm (¼ yd) of 90 cm (36 in) width material in a light colour, for pattern pieces B and E

20 cm (¼ yd) of 90 cm (36 in) width material, for pattern piece C

15 cm (6 in) of 90 cm (36 in) material, for pattern piece D

55 cm (21 in) of 120 cm (48 in) width furnishing-weight cotton in contrasting colours, for background

Tracing paper, thick card, metal ruler and handicraft knife for making templates

Thick paper for making paper linings

1.60 m (1¾ yd) piping cord

The Sunburst design dates from before 1850 and has many variations. On the coast it was known as Mariner's Compass, and inland it was also called the Sunflower. Many of the simpler versions were heavily padded and quilted, with the flower centre raised and surrounded by tightly stuffed petals. It can be made either by the piecing or the appliqué method. The finished cushion measures 45 cm x 45 cm (18 in x 18 in).

Templates

Trace the pattern pieces from page 63 and make one cardboard template of each. It is essential that the templates are completely accurate or the sharp angles of the patches will not fit together well.

Place the templates on the wrong side of the material, with one edge in line with the grain of the fabric. Draw round each shape, leaving 8 mm (¼ in) all round for turnings (**1**).

Using the same templates, cut the paper linings. It is best to draw round each one before cutting out. Fit the papers together on a board to check that they fit perfectly.

1 Cut out the fabric patches. Use a fairly stiff paper for the linings to prevent the points becoming bent.

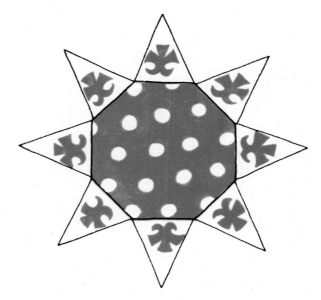

2 Join the first ring of patches to the centre octagon. When you are adding the remaining patches, always stitch towards the point where the angles meet.

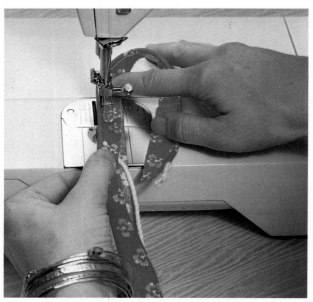

3 Cover the piping cord with the bias material and machine close to the cord. Use a zipper foot.

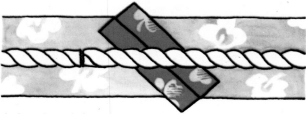

4 Cut the piping cord to the exact length and join with a latex glue. Seam the ends of the bias strip.

5 The basic Sunburst design can be made up in different colours and appliquéd to the background.

Patchwork

Make up each patch (see page 12), taking great care at the points.

Starting with the centre patch and with right sides together, join the first ring of patches (shape B) to each side of octagon A (2). Add remaining patches one ring at a time, following sequence B-E. Always stitch towards the point where angles meet to ensure a snug fit. Do not trim any excess fabric at the outer points. (Do this later when the patchwork is mounted.)

Press patchwork on wrong side. Remove tacking threads. Press on right side before removing papers.

To mount patchwork

Fold furnishing material in half. Cut. Centre the Sunburst carefully on the right side of one of these pieces. Pin and tack in position. Blindstitch in place (see page 13), using a matching thread. When working round each point, trim off most of the excess fabric and use your needle to push the remainder in under the patch.

Trim the completed work down to a square 49 cm x 49 cm ($18\frac{1}{2}$ in x $18\frac{1}{2}$ in). Cut the back of the cushion cover to match.

Corded piping

Wash the piping cord to shrink. From remaining fabric in main colour, cut 4 cm ($1\frac{1}{2}$ in) wide strips on the bias. Join the strips to 180 cm (76 in) in length. Cover the cord with the strip of material. Sew close to cord, using a zipper foot on the machine (3).

With raw edges together, pin the piping to the right side of the patchwork square. Make curves at all four corners. Tack in place. Leave 8 cm (3 in) free at either end.

Cut the cord with a 1.5 cm ($\frac{1}{2}$ in) overlap and splice the two ends together. Alternatively cut them to the exact length and stick with a latex glue. Match the ends of the bias strip and seam them together (4). Tack the remaining cord inside the binding and pin to the patchwork. Still using the zipper foot, machine all round close to the bound cord.

To complete cushion

With right sides together, pin front and back of cushion cover together. Machine close to cord, leaving a 25 cm (10 in) opening on one side. Trim corners and clip curves. Turn to right side. Insert cushion and slipstitch opening.

Diamond Pattern Yoke
to adapt to your own pattern

1 Lay out the patches as designed on the tracing. Working diagonally from left to right, machine them into strips. Press all seams open as you work.

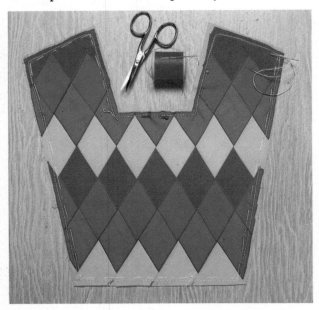

2 Using the pattern piece, cut out the patchwork yoke and lining. Pin the two together and tack all round. You can now treat them as a single layer.

You will need:
Commercial dress pattern, with separate yoke
Yellow dressweight cotton (see pattern)
20 cm ($\frac{1}{4}$ yd) each of red, blue and green cotton
30 cm ($\frac{1}{3}$ yd) of fine cotton lining
Tracing paper, thick card, metal ruler and handicraft knife, for making template

Trace the 4 cm ($1\frac{1}{2}$ in) diamond from page 10. Using this as your guide for the inside measurement, construct a window template from thick card (see page 11). Allow 7 mm ($\frac{1}{4}$ in) seam allowance all round.

Take a tracing of the yoke (or whatever section of the pattern is to be made up in patchwork). Using your template and working from the centre outwards, draw the arrangement of patches onto the tracing. Make a note on each patch of the colour it is to be and refer to this later. The number of patches of each colour can be estimated from this drawing. Make the patchwork at least 2.5 cm (1 in) larger than the original pattern piece to allow for cutting out.

Using your window template and drawing both a cutting and stitching line, cut the required number of patches from each colour. Lay them out ready to assemble. Machine into strips (1).

Working from bottom right to top left, machine the strips together. Be careful to match the points. Press all seams open as you work, then press the whole section. Lay the yoke pattern on the patchwork, matching centres. Cut out. Staystitch all round 3 mm ($\frac{1}{8}$ in) from the edge (2).

Using the same pattern piece, cut a lining. With wrong sides facing, pin the. lining and patchwork together. Catch the two fabrics at regular intervals with tiny stitches on the wrong side. Tack all round (2).

The garment can now be made up, the patchwork section being treated as a single layer. To reduce bulk, replace any arm and neck facings that overlap the patchwork section with a bias binding cut from one of the materials.

Block Quilt
with Lone Star and Windmill motifs

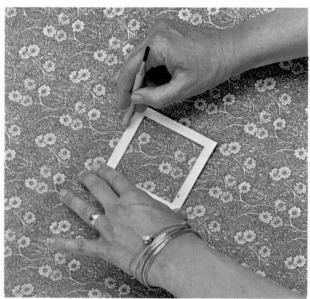

1 Cut the patches with the aid of your template, marking both the cutting and stitching line. Always cut on the straight grain of the fabric.

2 Arrange the patches round the centre square before sewing them into strips. Return each strip to its position on the board.

You will need:
3.50 m (5½ yd) of 90 cm (36 in) width natural calico
9.50 m (10 yd) of 90 cm (36 in) width assorted cotton prints in toning colours (choose five light shades and five dark)
6.75 m (7¾ yd) of 97 cm (38 in) width lightweight terylene wadding
6.90 m (8 yd) of 90 cm (36 in) width dressweight cotton lining
1 m (1 yd) of 90 cm (36 in) width matching or contrasting fabric, for binding quilt edge
Thick card, metal ruler and handicraft knife, for making templates
Two skeins *coton à broder* No. 18, or crochet cotton (not synthetic cotton), for knotting

This design is based on the American block quilt. Each block is constructed separately and when finished is 42 cm (18 in) square. Thirty blocks are required to make a double-bed sized quilt. **N.B.** The metric-size quilt is smaller than the imperial-size quilt. Remember to follow one set of measurements only throughout.

The design is very simple and, although it combines both piecing and appliqué techniques, it lends itself to machine sewing as no paper patterns are used in the main part of the quilt.

The patches are arranged round a plain calico centre. A separately constructed motif is appliquéd on afterwards. Pre-shrink all fabric.

Templates
Make a square window template from card or plastic, with an outer size 9 cm (3½ in) square and inner size 7 cm (3 in) square.

Each block requires:
One 30 cm (13 in) square of natural calico
Ten 9 cm (3½ in) square patches cut from a mixture of light fabrics
Ten 9 cm (3½ in) square patches cut from a mixture of dark fabrics

Cut the patches with the aid of your template, marking both the cutting and stitching lines (**1**).

To make one block

Arrange the patches round the centre square, alternating light and dark colours.

Using the drawn lines as a guide, stitch the six patches which form each side of the block together into two strips. Repeat with the top and bottom row of patches, seaming them into strips of four (2).

With right sides together, pin and sew the top strip of four patches to the central square. Repeat with the bottom strip, making sure that the stitching lines are 28 cm (12 in) apart. Open outwards and press.

With right sides together, seam one strip of six patches to the left side of the block, joining up with the edges of the squares at the top and bottom. Repeat with the remaining strip of six patches on the right side of the block, once again checking that the stitching lines are 28 cm (12 in) apart. Open outwards and press well.

Mark the top left-hand corner of each block with a coloured thread.

Appliqué motifs

These are made up separately and appliquéd onto each block before the quilt is pieced together. Here two motifs have been used in a variety of arrangements. Fifteen repeats of each motif were made and placed alternately all over the quilt.

Windmill

Cut two 10 cm (4½ in) square patches from light material, and two 10 cm (4½ in) square patches from dark material.

Cut all four patches diagonally into triangles and group them alternately in light and dark pairs (3a).

With right sides together, pin and sew one light and one dark triangle together, leaving a 1 cm (¼ in) seam allowance. Repeat with the other three pairs of triangles. Press all the seams open as you go. Join the squares into pairs (3b), then into one square (3c).

Trim excess material away at the corners. Turn under 1 cm (¼ in) all round. Tilt the motif onto its point and tack it to the centre of the block. Blindstitch in position (see page 13).

Lone Star

Cut one patch 14 cm (5½ in) square, then cut two 6 cm (3½ in) square patches from light material, and two 6 cm (3½ in) square patches from dark material.

Cut all four small patches diagonally into

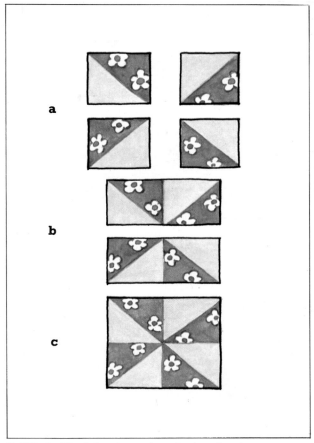

3 Windmill: join the pairs of triangles into squares before making up into one unit.

4 The Lone Star pieces laid out ready for making up. This pattern is also called Saw Tooth Star.

triangles and arrange them alternately, light and dark, round the centre square (**4**).

To make the paper linings, cut one piece of paper 12 cm (5 in) square and four pieces 6 cm (2½ in) square. Cut the small pieces diagonally to form triangles.

Make up as for ordinary patchwork. Appliqué to centre of block, using blindstitch (**5**).

5 When you blindstitch the Lone Star to the block, use your needle to push the excess fabric under each point. You may need to trim the corners first.

6 Edge the quilt with a contrasting binding. You can embroider your name and the date in one corner.

To complete the quilt

Press all the completed blocks and lay them out on the bed so that you can see the design before you sew them together.

Using a 1 cm (¼ in) seam, join all the blocks of one row across the quilt. Press the seams as you go, for once the whole patchwork is assembled it will be more difficult to handle.

Tack and sew the rows of blocks together.

Lining and interlining (see page 14)

Cut the terylene wadding into three equal lengths and join them with herringbone stitch. The seams will run horizontally across the quilt.

Cut the cotton lining into three and make it up 5 cm (2 in) larger than the patchwork top. (If you are following the imperial measurements, you may find that you need to add an extra 6 in strip to the width of the lining. This has been allowed for in the estimated material.)

Join all three thicknesses together. Leave in the tacking stitches.

Knotting

This is a very simple alternative to quilting. All three thicknesses of the quilt are held together by a reef knot tied on the underside.

Lay the quilt out flat and pin through all thicknesses at the four corners of each block. Turn over to the wrong side and, using *coton a broder* (or crotchet cotton), take a stitch through the lining and wadding which just catches the excess material at the corners of the patchwork blocks. This stitch should not be visible on the right side. Take a second stitch over the first, pull tight and tie the ends in a reef knot. Using the same method, make a knot at various points all over the quilt, following the lines of the patchwork design, about every 14–21 cm (6–9 in) apart. Remove the tacking threads.

Binding

Cut 5 cm (2 in) wide strips on the bias. Join them together to the required length, approximately 10 m (11 yd).

With right sides together, tack the binding to the edge of the quilt, leaving a 1 cm (½ in) seam allowance. Machine through all four thicknesses. Trim off excess wadding and lining.

Turn the binding over to the wrong side. Turn under a 1 cm (½ in) seam allowance and hem down. Mitre the corners (**6**).

Rainbow Quilt
with appliqué flowers and butterflies

You will need:

Of 90 cm (36 in) width material:
30 cm (12 in) in buttercup yellow
10 cm (4 in) in orange
10 cm (4 in) in pale pink
1 m (1 yd) in shocking pink
50 cm (18 in) in pale mauve
50 cm (18 in) in purple
1 m (1 yd) in sky blue
50 cm (18 in) in pale green
50 cm (18 in) in dark leaf green
1.50 m (1½ yd) of 90 cm (36 in) width dress-weight cotton lining in a bright colour
1.50 m (1½ yd) of 97 cm (38 in) width lightweight terylene wadding
Tracing paper, thick card, metal ruler and handicraft knife, for making template

This child's quilt uses all the colours of the spectrum and is quickly made up on the machine.

It is approximately 85 cm x 125 cm (2 ft 10 in x 4 ft), but the size can be adjusted by adding

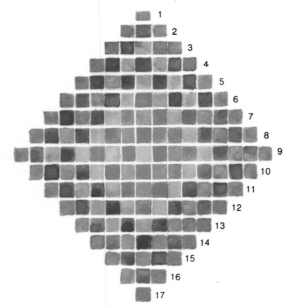

1 Colour guide for the centre block. Join the patches into 17 strips and seam together.

coloured strips of fabric at the top and bottom.

The flowers and butterflies are constructed separately and can be made from any combination of colours used in the quilt. They are lightly padded so that they stand out in relief, and are sewn in place by hand using a loosely worked slipstitch which catches only the underside of each padded part.

Template

Make one square window template from card or plastic, with an outer size 7 cm (2½ in) square and inner size 5 cm (2 in) square (see page 11).

Centre block

Cut the coloured patches for the centre of the quilt with the aid of your template, marking both the cutting and stitching lines. Always cut across the *width* of the material so that there will be sufficient left for the edging strips to be cut in one piece.

The number of patches required is: 1 yellow, 4 orange, 8 pale pink, 12 shocking pink, 16 pale mauve, 20 purple, 24 sky blue, 28 pale green and 32 dark green.

Using the colour chart (**1**) as a guide, arrange the patches in 17 lines ready for sewing. Beginning with line 2 and working from left to right, join the patches into a strip (see pages 13–14), leaving a 1 cm (¼ in) seam allowance. Press all seams open as you go. Repeat through to line 16. When complete seam all the strips together, working from top to bottom (1–17). Press well.

Cut two 44 cm (18 in) square pieces from sky blue material. Cut both squares diagonally in half, making four triangles. With right sides together, pin and sew the long sides of two of the triangles to opposite edges of the centre block. The seams will cut across all the points of the outer line of dark green patches. Repeat with the two remaining triangles, sewing through all thicknesses where the triangles meet. Open out into a square and press. Trim any excess corners.

Strips

Cut two 7 cm x 85 cm (2¾ in x 34 in) strips from the pale green, sky blue, pale mauve and purple materials. With right sides together and leaving a 1 cm (⅜ in) seam allowance, pin and sew four strips to one side of the centre block. Start with pale green and work outwards through sky blue and purple, finishing with light mauve at the edge. Repeat with the remaining four strips on the opposite side of the quilt. Press all seams outwards.

FLOWERS AND BUTTERFLIES

Trace off the shapes given and make paper patterns. Always pin the paper patterns to the wrong side of the fabric.

Draw round each pattern the specified number of times, using a soft pencil. *Allow a 5 mm (¼ in) seam allowance all round when cutting.* The pencil line will then act as your stitching guide.

Sunflower

Centre. From yellow material cut a circle 9 cm (3½ in) in diameter. Turn in 5 mm (¼ in) all round by pressing.

Petals. Cut ten from yellow material (**2**). With right sides together, stitch all round the curved edge, leaving the straight side open. Turn to right side, stuff lightly with terylene wadding and close opening.

Stamens. Make five. Take a scrap of yellow fabric, approximately 7 cm (2½ in) square. Place a thumbnail ball of wadding in the centre and fold over tightly. Secure with a stitch and make a shank by winding the thread round the neck several times (**3**). Finish off with backstitch.

Stalk. Cut a rectangle 6 cm x 8 cm (2¼ in x 3 in) from pale green fabric. Press in one long edge. Place the yellow stamen with shank innermost on this and roll up tightly into a stalk (**3**). Turn in raw edge and hem. Secure the two parts by taking a few stitches right through all thicknesses at the top of the stalk.

Pin and sew the petals and stamens in position (**4**), using backstitch along the raw edges. Place the centre circle over these edges and appliqué on in closely worked blindstitch (see page 13).

Leaves. Make five. Cut six light green and four dark green leaf shapes (**5**). Cut five leaf shapes from wadding. With right sides together, place

2 SUNFLOWER PETALS CUT 10 / SMALL CUPFLOWER CUT 2

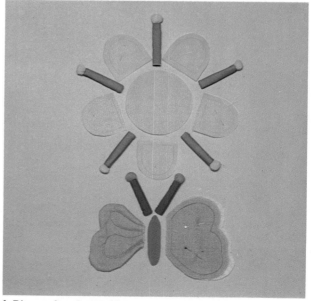

3 Making the stamens and the antennae.

4 Pieces for the sunflower and the butterfly.

a matching pair of fabric leaves on top of one wadding shape. Stitch all round through all thicknesses, leaving a 2 cm (1 in) gap on one side. Turn right sides out and close the gap with slipstitch. Work a straight machine stitch along the vein lines as shown on the pattern.

Bellflower

Make one (**6**). Construct the bellflower and stamens by the same method as the sunflower.

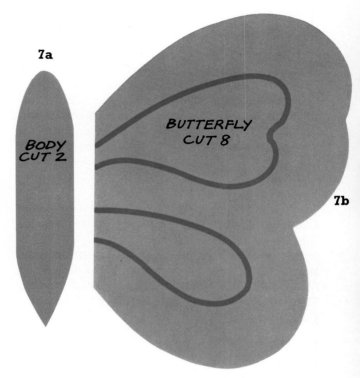

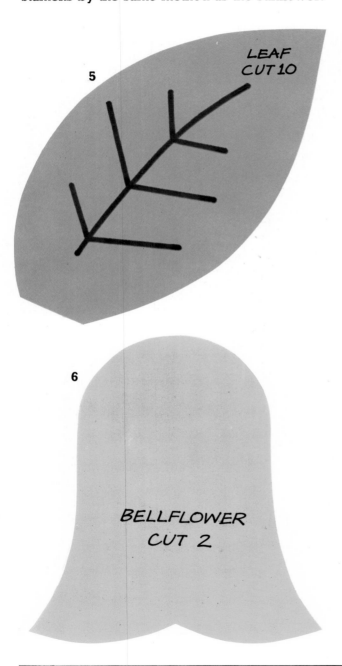

Secure the stamens with backstitch and the flower and two leaves with slipstitch.

Butterflies

Make two, one shocking pink and one pale mauve. Cut two pairs of wing shapes from material and two wing shapes from wadding (**7b**). With right sides together, place two wing shapes on top of one piece of wadding. Stitch all round, leaving the straight side open. Turn to the right side and work a machine stitch in contrasting cotton along the wing lines, as shown on the pattern. Repeat with the second wing.

Make two antennae in contrasting fabric. These are made exactly as the stamens for the sunflower.

Cut one body piece (**7a**). Backstitch the antennae in place. Place the body over the raw edges of the wings and antennae (**4**) and machine in place, using a fine zigzag stitch.

Globe flowers

From yellow material, cut two circles 5 cm (2 in) and two circles 6.5 cm (2¾ in) in diameter. Cut two matching circles from wadding. Assemble as described above, leaving a 2 cm

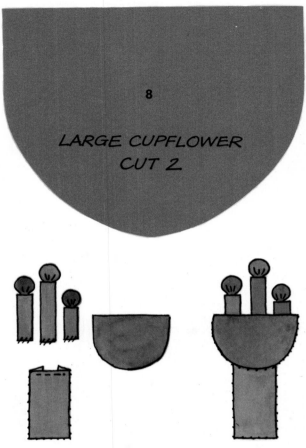

8

LARGE CUPFLOWER
CUT 2

9 Sew the stalk and stamens in place. Appliqué the flower over the raw edges to lie flat.

(1 in) gap for turning. Turn and close, making a flat seam at the base. Slipstitch in place.

From green material, cut two rectangles for stalks, 3.5 cm x 6 cm (1½ in x 2½ in) and 3.5 cm x 11 cm (1½ in x 4½ in). Turn in 5 mm (¼ in) all round and appliqué in position.

Cupflowers
Cut two of each size (**2, 8**) from a mixture of the pink and mauve materials. Turn in 5 mm (¼ in) all round. Make stamens and stalks to match, as described above. Backstitch the stamens in place (**9**) and appliqué the flowers over them so that they lie flat.

To complete the quilt
Cut interlining and backing to size and make up (see page 14).

Make two knots on the underside of the quilt at the top and bottom of the centre square to hold all thicknesses together (see page 50).

Cut the binding from the remaining shocking pink material and make up (see page 50).

Variation
The centre block can be extended to fit any size bed. Simply add more rows of patches, alternating the light and dark colours with each row. Make the patchwork up to the required width and then turn it into a square by adding plain fabric at the four corners.

10 Sew the flowers and leaves in place by hand, catching only the underside of each padded part.

11 The butterflies and flowers can be made from any combination of colours used in the quilt.

Patchwork Annie
nightdress case in dog's tooth patchwork

You will need:

Dressweight cotton scraps, in assorted colours
1 m (1 yd) of 90 cm (36 in) width dressweight cotton, for plain patches, lining and base
Scraps of natural calico, for head and arms
125 g (4 oz) of kapok, for stuffing
50 g (2 oz) chunky knitting wool, for hair
20 cm (8 in) strip of seam binding or tape
Scraps of coloured felt and embroidery thread
Tracing paper, thick card, metal ruler and handicraft knife, for making template
Latex glue

Making the doll

Trace the pattern from page 58. From natural calico, cut two head pieces on the bias and two pairs of arms on the grain. Mark darts round the head on the wrong side of both pieces. Trace the features onto the right side of one piece.

Fold and stitch darts along dotted lines. With right sides together, machine head and body, leaving base seam open. Clip at neck. Turn to right side and stuff firmly. Turn in and oversew base seam. Using double thread, take a running stitch round neck. Pull tight and secure.

Arms With right sides facing and leaving a 7 mm ($\frac{1}{4}$ in) seam, stitch round edge, leaving top open. Clip at thumb. Turn and stuff to within 2.5 cm (1 in) of top. Fold top of arm, making a point and secure through all thicknesses. Sew arm to body of doll, matching point of arm to the shoulder and stitching 2.5 cm (1 in) on either side of shoulder point.

Face Using a single thread and a fine chain stitch, embroider eyelashes and mouth. Cut two felt circles for eyes and glue in place. Colour cheeks and nose with a smudge of lipstick, and seal with a hot iron through tissue paper.

Hair Cut a piece of card 23 cm x 18 cm (9 in x 7 in). Wind the wool evenly round the card lengthways. Pass the strip of tape under the wool and backstitch wool and tape together to make a 15 cm (6 in) parting. Turn over the card and cut through wool at centre to remove.

Reinforce parting on machine.

Pin wool to doll's head where marked on pattern and backstitch along parting. Tie hair in bunches and trim ends.

Patchwork dress

Trace the pyramid triangle from page 10 and transfer to card. To construct a window template, draw a 1 cm ($\frac{3}{8}$ in) seam all round. Using a sharp knife and metal ruler, cut out the template along both the inside and outside lines (see page 11).

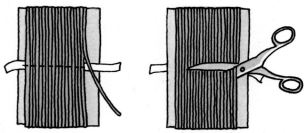

1 Wind the wool round the card and backstitch the tape underneath. Turn over the card and cut wool.

2 As each triangle is added, match the drawn points of the stitching lines with a pin.

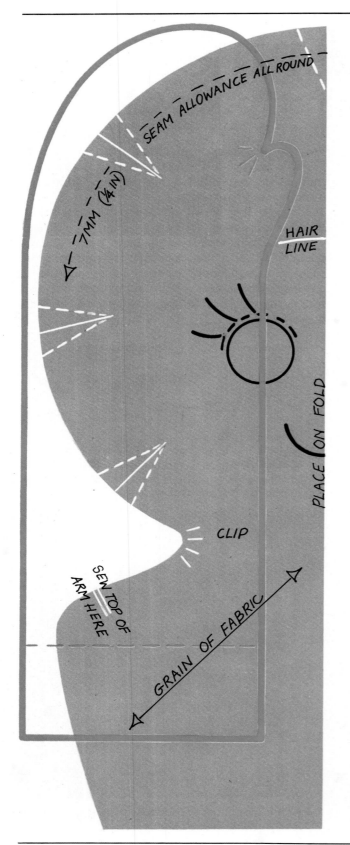

Using your template as a guide and marking both cutting and stitching lines on the wrong side, cut 52 print patches and 48 plain patches, always keeping one long edge on the grain. Arrange the patches on a board in four lines of 25, alternating print and plain triangles.

Beginning with the top line and working from left to right, join the patches into a strip (2). Press seams open. Trim corners. Working from top to bottom, sew the four strips together to make one piece. Press seams one way. Turn down a 1 cm (⅜ in) strip to wrong side on each short edge of the patchwork. Tack in place. Trim excess material.

Finishing doll
Feet Trace pattern 2 from page 53, adding on a 5 mm (³⁄₁₆ in) seam allowance. Cut four from felt. Leaving a 5 mm (³⁄₁₆ in) seam, machine the two shapes together round the curved edge. Turn and stuff lightly. Centre the feet 7 cm (3 in) apart, facing inwards at the bottom of the skirt. Tack in place.
Base Draw an oval on paper, 27 cm x 22 cm (10¾ in x 8½ in) in diameter. Cut two ovals from plain fabric. Mark centre front and back of long sides. With right sides facing, pin skirt to base, matching centre front and back. Ease fullness on curves. Check feet. Sew in place and turn to right side.
Lining Cut a rectangle 81 cm x 37 cm (32 in x 14½ in) from plain fabric. Join to base as for skirt. With wrong sides facing, drop lining into skirt. Match edges. Slipstitch in place all round back opening.
Waistband Cut a piece of fabric 6 cm x 26 cm (2½ in x 10 in). Fold in half lengthways. On wrong side, stitch across ends. Turn. With right sides facing, gather skirt to waistband in tiny pleats. Machine. Turn under raw edge. Hem.
Straps For each strap, cut a piece of fabric 12 cm x 5 cm (4½ in x 2 in) and an edging strip 5 cm x 16 cm (2 in x 6½ in). Narrowly hem three sides of edging strip. Gather raw edge up to 7 cm (2¾ in). With right sides facing, centre frill on strap. Stitch. Turn under raw edge and sew down.

Sew straps to waistband at centre 2.5 cm (1 in) apart. Fit dress on doll. Adjust length of straps at back so dress fits snugly under arms. Sew in place. Make two 30 cm (12 in) ties and stitch to waistband. Catch waistband to doll's body under arms.

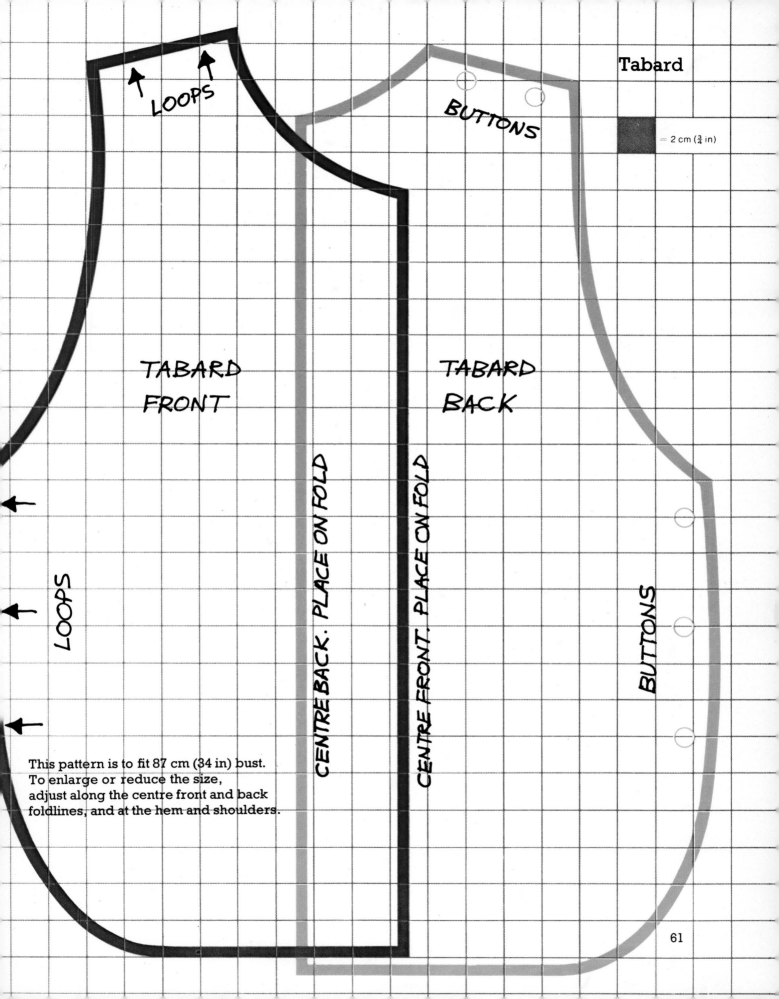

Tabard

LOOPS

BUTTONS

= 2 cm (¾ in)

TABARD
FRONT

TABARD
BACK

CENTRE BACK. PLACE ON FOLD

CENTRE FRONT. PLACE ON FOLD

LOOPS

BUTTONS

This pattern is to fit 87 cm (34 in) bust.
To enlarge or reduce the size,
adjust along the centre front and back
foldlines, and at the hem and shoulders.

61

House-on-the-Hill Bag

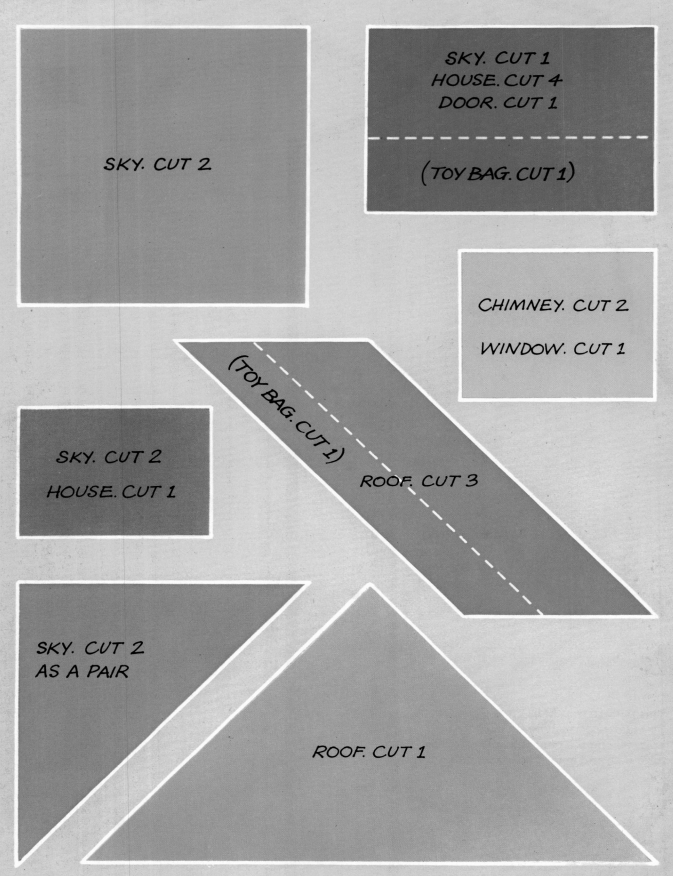

SKY. CUT 2

SKY. CUT 1
HOUSE. CUT 4
DOOR. CUT 1

(TOY BAG. CUT 1)

CHIMNEY. CUT 2

WINDOW. CUT 1

SKY. CUT 2
HOUSE. CUT 1

(TOY BAG. CUT 1)

ROOF. CUT 3

SKY. CUT 2
AS A PAIR

ROOF. CUT 1

No seam allowance given. Allow 1 cm (½ in) all round each section.

Also cut one section 32 cm x 9.5 cm (12½ in x 4 in) of flowered material for the hill.

Sunburst Cushion

List of Suppliers

Cotton fabrics
John Lewis
Oxford Street
London W1A 1EX

(branches)
Peter Jones
Sloane Square
London SW1W 8EL

John Barnes
Finchley Road
London NW3 6LJ

Jones Brothers
Holloway Road
London N7 6NY

Pratts
Streatham High Road
London SW16 1BD

Caleys
High Street
Windsor SL4 1LL

Heelas
Broad Street
Reading RG1 2BB

Trewin Brothers
Queens Road
Watford WD1 2LQ

Bainbridge
Market Street
Newcastle-upon-Tyne
NE99 1AB

Cole Brothers
Barkers Pool
Sheffield S1 1EP

George Henry Lee
Basnet Street
Liverpool L1 1EA

Jessops
Victoria Centre
Nottingham NG1 3QA

Robert Sayle
St Andrew's Street
Cambridge CB2 3BL

Tyrell and Green
Above Bar
Southampton SO9 5HU

Knight and Lee
Palmerston Road
Southsea PO5 3QE

John Lewis
St James Centre
Edinburgh EH1 3SP

Standen Fabrics
Wimbledon Chase
Station Buildings
London SW20

(branches)
14 Kingshade Walk
Epsom
Surrey

32 Fife Road
Kingston
Surrey

68 Chapel Street
Penzance
Cornwall

Laura Ashley Limited
40 Sloane Street
London SW1

(branches)
71-73 Lower Sloane Street
London SW3

157 Fulham Road
London SW3

12 New Bond Street
Bath
Avon

1a Queens Circus
Montpelier
Cheltenham
Gloucestershire

17-19 Watergate Row
Chester
Cheshire

10 Spittal Street
Edinburgh
Midlothian

404 Byres Road
Glasgow
Lanarkshire

30 Great Oak Street
Llanidloes
Powys
Wales

58 Bridesmith Gate
Nottingham
Nottinghamshire

26-27 Little Clarendon
Street
Oxford

3-5 Dove Street
Norwich
Norfolk

*and at most Singer
shops*

Felt
The Felt and Hessian Shop
34 Greville Street
London EC1

Furnishing fabrics
John Lewis (see above)

Sanderson Fabrics
56 Berner Street
London W1

(branches)
70 Drury Lane
Birmingham

Black Boy Road
Exeter
Devon

Silks, satin, lurex
Borovick Fabrics Limited
16 Berwick Street
London W1V 1EX

Templates
The Needlewoman Shop
146-148 Regent Street
London W1

FURTHER READING
Doris E. Marston *Patchwork Today* G. Bell and Sons
Limited, London, 1968
Averil Colby *Patchwork Quilts* Batsford, London, 1975
Sheila Betterton *American Textiles and Needlework*
American Museum in Britain, Bath, Somerset

Margeurite Ickis *The Standard Book of Quilt Making
and Collecting* Dover Publications Inc., New York, 1949
Ruby S. McKim *101 Patchwork Patterns* Dover
Publications Inc., New York, 1962

ACKNOWLEDGMENTS
The publishers gratefully acknowledge the assistance
and co-operation of:
The American Museum in Britain, Claverton Manor,
Bath, Avon (page 33)
Aquila Gift Shop, Gate Street, London WC1 (page 35)
Covent Garden Cycles, 41 Shorts Gardens, London
WC2 (page 29)
E. P. Dutton Publishers, New York and America Hurrah
Antiques, New York (page 9)

Galt Toys, 30 Great Marlborough Street, London W1
(pages 41 and 59)

Heal's Sleep Shop, Heal's, 196 Tottenham Court Road,
London W1 (page 43)

Laura Ashley Limited (see addresses above) (page 29)
Quilt Gallery, Inc., U.S.A. (page 6)

Sewing machines by courtesy of The Singer Company
(U.K.) Ltd